Samsung Galaxy S3
The Definitive Samsung S3 User Guide

Discover EVERYTHING the new Samsung S3 has to offer, including exciting Tips and Tricks, with this Samsung S3 Manual

By Francis Monico

Table of Contents

Introduction: The Samsung Galaxy S3

Welcome! If you are a new user of the Galaxy S3, you will likely have a lot of questions. This isn't a surprise, considering it is the most complex and impressive Galaxy model to date. Samsung and Android were meticulous in enhancing old features, involving new features, and providing an unprecedented user experience.

What You Will Learn

You will learn the new and old features of this Galaxy model; additionally you'll learn some tips and tricks to use your Galaxy in ways you probably have never tried before.

The best way to understand the complex abilities of your new phone is to learn of all the Galaxy S2 capabilities in addition to the new functions included with the new model. We will specifically annotate the features that are new to the S3 to ensure you understand the full suite of features and functionalities. There are features that allow you to use your phone as more than a phone that the average user may not notice.

Learning about your S3's hardware will help you understand the graphics and processor. You'll also learn how to sync your phone with your computer, which is being used as a huge productivity boost among customers. The top apps for the S3 will be on display to help you start your Android use off correctly, and you'll even learn about accessories, why the S3 is better than the iPhone 5, and the new Samsung Mini S3.

On top of everything that has already been listed, you'll also be learning some bonus tips and tricks to improve upon your S3 usage and make it your new darling, muse and overall favorite tool.

Improvements over the Galaxy S2

In the fast moving world of mobile technology new devices are sometimes very quickly superseded by their successors. However it came as a surprise to many when 2011's Android product, the Galaxy S2, was updated just a year after its launch. However, the Galaxy S3 was well received by the tech crowd and users alike as it improved on all of Galaxy S2's features in such a short time frame.

What is even more astounding is how much future proofing has been built into the Galaxy S3. At the moment both the S2 and S3 are on the eve of being updated to the latest version of Android: Android Jellybean. The fact that the S2 is able to handle such a powerful operating system speaks volumes of the infinitely more powerful Galaxy S3 and the very long shelf life that is predicted for the super phone. So let's look into some of the advantages of owning the newer version of the phone.

Advantage 1: A Better Screen

The most common first impressions of the S3 are usually based upon the sheer size and clarity of the screen. Bigger is certainly better and infinitely more beautiful when you compare the S2 screen with its newer iteration. An extra half-inch has been added on the newer model to bump it up to a visually impressive 4.8 inches.

What is even more astounding is that the pixel count (the resolution of the screen; more obviously being better) has increased to such an extent. Last year's device had a screen resolution of 800x480 pixels; this year we see a vast improvement at 1280x720 pixels, pushing the screen into true HD territory. The new screen is a Super Amoled Plus; again an improvement over the original Super Amoled screen with brighter sharper colors and excellent power saving capability.

Advantage 2: A Better Battery

With a larger screen and faster processors than the S2, the S3 needed a better battery; Samsung has delivered. Both batteries are Lithium Ion batteries, providing just the right power to longevity ratio needed of a cutting edge device. However, the not insubstantial 1,650 mAh battery of the S2 is overshadowed by the 2,100 mAh of the S3.

This simply means the battery has more power to keep the mobile device working for longer. In the S3's case, that's a whole lot longer with 800 hours of Standby time compared to 620 hours and a very lengthy 22 hours talk time as opposed to only 9 hours. That's almost double the talk time and many users report that having a Galaxy S3 means that the nightly charging routine can be postponed to a day and a half or even two days of reasonable use before the battery needs recharging.

Advantage 3: A Camera of Note

Despite both of the devices having an 8-megapixel-rear camera, the S3 carries extra optimizations that make the newer version a highly respectable photo-taking device. The camera is quicker to access and uses its superior software to enable better photos to be taken. And that's even before we start to mention the multitude of extra features that have been crammed into the new camera. Now, if you want to capture HD video with the front facing camera you can, a feature that many S2 users would have loved to have.

Advantage 4: As Powerful as a Laptop? Galaxy S3's Impressive Hardware

The Galaxy S2 provides quite a powerful processer. Its dual core Arm Cortex A9 processor blitzes out to 1.2 GHz meaning that there are virtually no apps or games that will cause the handset to break down. With that being said, the new S3 is easily comparable to some laptops out today.

The Samsung Galaxy S3 boasts a Quad Core Processor (Exynos 4412 in some versions of the device) and runs at 1.4 GHz. This means that at the time of writing and for the foreseeable future, the S3 will easily meet all of your mobile processing needs.

Let's look at comparisons of the RAM between the S2 and S3. Random access memory (RAM) influences the ability of a computer chip to keep data that needs to be used and is a great measure of how fast a device can perform tasks. The S2 has 1,024 MB of RAM and the Samsung was able to double that number by providing the S3 with 2,048 MB of RAM.

This is one of the most significant upgrades. Software and mobile developers now have the ability to create the most powerful and demanding apps, games, and software for this mobile device. With such expansive RAM now made accessible to everyday users, there will be a surge of new applications arriving made purposely for the S3.

Advantage 5: Why We Need 4G Phones

4G Mobile Data connections are simply the future of using Mobiles to connect to the Internet. 3G is the current standard (and before that 2 and 2.5G). It is a new standard of connecting devices to the Internet wirelessly and will provide improved Data Rates. With 4G readily available, it is not only possible connect more speedily to the Internet, but downloading movies and other media becomes possible.

This is clearly one area in which the new mobile is far superior to its predecessor. The Samsung Galaxy S3 is one of the few mobile phones that will support 4G (LTE) networks.

Advantage 6: Even More Reasons To Own a Galaxy S3

The Galaxy S3, with its brushed polycarbonate body, is available in Pebble Blue, Marble White and Garnet Red colors. There are rumors of Amber brown, Titanium grey and Sapphire black being available in the future too. This modern day powerful phone is thus quickly becoming something of a style icon.

Features and Functions of the Galaxy S3

If you own the Galaxy S3 or are considering purchasing one, there may be features that you know about, but don't fully understand. There may even be functions that you don't know about that could transform the way you use this device to better your everyday life. In this chapter, we aim to improve your understanding of the phone's features and discuss this device and its capabilities more in-depth.

The Camera

One of the top features of the S3's camera will prove a boon to those who rely on their mobile phone to take photographs. Traditionally, a mobile phone's camera is quite slow to start up and often-great photo opportunities are missed because of this. That's not the case with this camera, as the powerful processing power can have the 8 megapixel camera up and running in under 4 seconds.

Like many other features found on this phone, the camera also has a handy shortcut: If the screen is locked and you touch it whilst simultaneously turning the phone into landscape mode the camera will instantly open up. Now, once the camera is up and running, the magic really begins.

The leap in quality from last generation to this one is exponential thanks to a tremendous amount of software optimization. Contrast and white balance levels are two features of the camera that benefit enormously from improved software, resulting in much richer, vivid photos. Aside from the obvious benefit of improved pictures, the amount of new features is mind-boggling and will be explored in-depth later on.

The rear camera is bolstered by an excellent front facing camera at 1.9 MP, and now has the ability to capture video in 720p resolution.

Camera Resolution: 8 MP with a resolution of 3264 x 2448

Other Camera Features: Geo-tagging, image stabilization, autofocus, touch focus, digital zoom, video recording (HD)

Screen Features

Samsung's advertising campaign heavily promoted the ' Smart Stay' capability of their flagship S3 handset. The fact that a mobile phone is now powerful enough to recognize a person's face is amazing. Samsung has taken this ability in a fascinating new direction with Smart stay.

Originally, with a screen timeout being selected the phone's screen would simply stay on, draining battery power. Even having a screen timeout option selected could prove rather irritating as the screen could quite easily timeout during movie watching or any other function that doesn't require you to be constantly touching the screen.

Using its powerful processor and some very smart software 'Smart Stay ' uses the front facing camera to detect whether you are watching the screen . The screen will turn off if you are not watching or stay on if you are, allowing you to keep on enjoying your movie in peace.

Face unlock also comes as a part of these features and you can now choose to unlock your phone by using your own face as a security feature. The phone will simply not unlock if it doesn't recognize you!

Auto-rotate screen is another useful feature. In normal use, you can often find yourself changing the phone from landscape to portrait orientation depending upon what you are doing. Auto rotate let's you turn on the ability to rotate the screen depending upon the phone's orientation.

The Keyboard

The out of the box functionality of the keyboard is quite impressive. If for some reason it does not suit your needs, the S3 easily allows download of any keyboard or input interface from the Google Play Market.

The stock keyboard comes with a variety of useful options. Predictive text input is present, but this device always seems to be one step ahead of the competition with extra features that just make life that easier. Continuous input is one of those features borrowed from some of the more popular premium apps in the Google Play store; initially apps like Swype brought continuous input to a handful of devices.

Now with the Galaxy S3 you've got access to that ability from the start. The keyboard has become intuitive and text can be entered by swiping from one letter to the next. The keyboard will predict the required words with surprising accuracy and even learn your habits. For example, if you always swipe the "i" instead of "o" key the continuous text will learn and compensate for this habit. Aside from the obvious benefit that having a "swipe keyboard" brings in saving time, it will make even the most jaded mobile user smile at the fun that can be had in swiping out even the toughest messages.

It's just as easy to change to a new keyboard: Go into Settings, tap on Language and input and then tap on Default. If you've downloaded a new keyboard you can make that your default.

Other features that make the phone easier to use include auto capitalization and auto punctuation. If you really want the ultimate in high-tech keyboard inputs you can use Google Voice to text to input text on the phone. You can speak your messages into your phone and they will be typed out!

The Samsung Galaxy S3's Display

When news of Samsung's newest phone broke, many commentators were surprised at the bold move of making a larger device instead as opposed to the more pocket friendly devices that seem to be the modern trend. Samsung's gamble to produce a 4.8-inch screen has paid off, as the display is one of the most immediately captivating features.

The resolution is better (or at least on par) with all major devices today. The Super Amoled Plus screen has a resolution of 1280 x 720 pixels and a pixel density of 309 pixels per inch. This translates to gorgeous looking games and media. This ultra sharp display is remarkable on a screen of this size and comes with a host of features to improve your experience.

Easily accessed from a drop down menu is the screen's auto brightness function that allows automatically adjusts the screen's brightness based on ambient lighting conditions. If you're in bright sunlight, the brightness increases to compensate and if you're indoors the brightness decreases, a very useful feature not just for battery life but also to reduce eyestrain associated with lengthy use of the screen.

For business users and those wanting to connect their devices to larger screens such as televisions or projectors, this phone has the ability to support an additional display. That means that if you want to display a PowerPoint presentation via a projector you can hook up your device and the display will be mirrored on both your phone and on the projector (or any other output device).

In addition to it's versatility and lightning quick speed, the display also has multi-touch capabilities. Thus, any apps that need to be controlled by two or more fingers are of supported. The screen uses scratch resistant glass called Corning Gorilla Glass 2, some of the most durable touch-screen glass on the market.

The Expanded Features of the Galaxy S3

Samsung has put a lot of thought into their mobile and made good on their tagline: "Designed for humans, inspired by nature". The overwhelming majority of reviews and consumers point out the brilliance of the phone and what makes every user happy, from the most experienced Smartphone user to those who've just unboxed their first device.

All agree the plethora of unique expanded features put the S3 in a class of it's own. These features are considered expanded features, as they are not necessarily functions that a novice owner will use on a daily basis, but once you're aware of them you'll never know how you got by without them.

NFC on the Galaxy S3

During the 2012 Olympics all Olympic athletes were given Galaxy S3s to use around London. Aside from the privilege of having cutting edge mobile devices, the athletes were also able to use the devices NFC capabilities to pay for small transactions. The phone essentially has an NFC chip that allows the device to communicate wirelessly at short distances with other NFC capable terminals. During the games the initial wave of contactless payment shops began to use the new technology of Near Field Communications (NFC).

Now there are a handful of shops that enable NFC payments, meaning that you can load money onto a contactless payment app and, like the Olympians, walk into a shop and pay with a swipe of your phone. As more and more shops start to use this technology, the NFC enabled device could realistically replace your wallet.

S-Beam

To make their flagship phone even easier and more intuitive, Samsung created S-Beam. Once an initial connection is set up with a friends device, all sorts of information such as pictures, contacts etc. can be exchanged by simply touching the back of one device to the other.

S-Voice

By double pressing on the S3's physical home button you can access the S-Voice function. Greeted by the phrase "What would you like to do?" this function opens up a whole new way of using your phone. Essentially S-Voice acts as your personal assistant, allowing you to set alarms, open up apps and perform a host of other functions. If you want to play music, simply request S-Voice to open up your music (and then have the ability to play, pause etc. with voice control). You can even request specific genres of music to be played!

The function is not just limited to activating phone functions, but also uses the enormous power of Google's search engines to make the S-Voice function a true guru for any requests and queries you choose to send its way. It's not just English speakers who can benefit as British, Italian, German, French, Spanish and Korean languages are supported.

Using the Camera to Share and Play

Aside from the many specialty functions of the camera that allow you to change everything from the white balance to saturation, there are other features that give more life to your photos. Whether you're using the camera's on-board editing tools to "cartoon" your photos or shooting stunning panoramic views, you'll have a variety of smart features to share and appreciate your photos even more.

Buddy photo share not only uses the Galaxy's superior processing power to tag and recognize faces on your photos but you'll also be able to link and share those photos either directly to your friends phones or via their social networks.

Samsung recognizes that social networks are important so it has revolutionized keeping up to date with your connections by inventing the social tag function. By easily linking your friends' photos to any of their social networks you'll be able to get updates when they change their status. All this by simply looking at their photo!

Motion Activated Features

Under the settings menu you can find a heading titled "Motion". Accessing this menu opens up a large range of motion activated features unique to this handset that have been designed with ease of use in-mind. All of the motion-activated features overcome the multiple button presses needed to accomplish what should be simple tasks. Once "Motion Activation" is selected you'll have the ability to:

- Direct Call - Just hold up the handset when you have a contact displayed on screen, whether that contact is displayed in your phone book or in a text message; all you need to do is hold your S3 to your ear and their number will automatically be dialed.

- Smart Alert is one of those simple ideas that really proves effective. Nearly every mobile phone displays a blinking LED light to show missed calls and indicate other alerts, but that's easy to miss especially if your phone screen is obscured in a case or out of site. Smart Alert will vibrate to alert you of new notifications.

- There are numerous occasions when "Turn over to mute/pause" will come in handy. If you don't want to take a call and hanging up will seem rude, or if you're fumbling around to turn your phone's alarm off in the dark then you'll appreciate the ability to easily turn your phone over to mute the sound.

- This phone can also distinguish gestures like palm swipes, which can be used to capture screen shots, and a simple touch of your palm can mute sounds.

- There are many other gestures, flicks, touches, wipes and movements that can be used to make life with your phone much simpler.

True Multitasking

We've already mentioned the powerful processor in this device, and at the moment developers are just starting to scratch the surface of how much can truly be achieved with this quad core engine. Out-of-the box, it allows easy multi tasking , as recently used apps are cached in the background and can be instantly activated with a quick button press.

Another very impressive feature is the "Pop up Play" feature: not only are you able to watch HD videos, but you can open the video in a window that you can float above another function. In other words, there's no need to stop watching your film when you need to send a text message, as you can easily do both at the same time!

Why Android and Touchwiz Work Well Together

The Samsung Galaxy S3 is an Android phone. What that means for the average user is that you will have access to one of the planet's fastest and slickest operating systems, the ability to customize features to your heart's content and access to the millions of apps on the Google Play Market.

However, Samsung has taken the standard Ice Cream Sandwich version of Android and overlaid it with their own "Touchwiz" interface. Essentially you'll be using an Android phone with a number of added features unique to the Galaxy S3 handset. The camera app with Touchwiz UX enables best-shot mode with virtually zero lag and burst shot mode (for action pictures such as sports shots). Other features include improved gallery and music apps.

One example of how the music app uses Touchwiz (reminding us again of how this phone is optimized for sharing) is that music can now be streamed to other devices on your network and shared by Bluetooth and email.

Additional features that promote sharing include Buddy photo share, which is the Touchwiz skinned gallery that allows you to view videos, music files and photos by time, location or person. In other words, you can sort the photos for easier access by just seeing those that are tagged with family member's names. This makes both viewing and sharing easier.

The Future of the Samsung Galaxy S3

Earlier we alluded to the phone's strong future, with its superior hardware and software capabilities that will make it a desirable device for some time to come. Already, throughout different regions, we are seeing the benefits of this. Most notably as the EE (Everything Everywhere) network in Europe expands 4G connectivity and more and more retail establishments adopt NFC forms of payment.

As an owner of an S3 these are exciting times; in the following months the already fantastic Android Ice -Cream Sandwich operating system is being updated to Android Jellybean. Naturally the S3 is one of the foremost mobiles that will be updated with Jellybean, bringing a smoother interface (nicknamed 'Project Butter' by Google for it's silky smoothness), improved notifications and menu organization as well as the very exciting "Google Now" function. This function further enhances Android's Personal Assistant functions by harnessing the power of Google's search.

"Google Now" will use all functions of your phone, from your email to GPS, to give you better search results and even give you new suggestions. For example, if Google Now sees that you commute every day, it can give you a pop up notice warning of a traffic jam without prompting! Samsung will enhance Jellybean further by adding its own Touchwiz ideas like the ability to resize the "Pop -Up Play " window and a 'Blocking Mode' for when you don't want to be disturbed. With a Samsung Galaxy S3 the future is always today!

Hardware: Processor and Graphics

The Samsung Galaxy S3 is by far one of the fastest mobile devices available today. This device comes with two slightly different specifications. The international version is powered by the Exynos 4 Quad SoC (System on a Chip). This new chip that Samsung has employed in their latest phone is reputed to have twice the performance and use 20 percent less power than the S2.

The other version is widely available in the American market; it has the advantage of being designed primarily to use 4G mobile connections. This 4G LTE version uses a Qualcomm Snapdragon S4 SoC. A 1.5 GHz Krait CPU. To find parity in the slightly differing versions of the CPU (Central Processing Unit), it was decided to launch the international version with 1Gb of RAM and the 4G LTE versions with 2Gb. Regardless of the CPU your S3 contains, both deliver great processing output.

Advantages of the S3's Superior Processor

One of the clear advantages of having a faster processor in a phone is that you can expect it to always perform swiftly and smoothly. The amount of power the S3 provides is unprecedented and easily comparable to the power of personal computers just several years back.

There are many apps, games and programs that will simply not work well, or at all, on a less powerful device. For example, playing high-definition video smoothly requires intensive hardware demands. The Galaxy S3 performs these types of functions very easily due to its powerful processor. In many benchmarking tests, the processing power of the S3 outshines most all other devices in its category. The most immediate advantage is the speed of which you are able to browse the Internet, as these speeds easily compare to using a desktop computer!

Many functions lag in other mobile devices. Everything from opening apps to making a telephone call is fairly slow. This is mostly due to the operating system of which the mobile device operates on. Whether a device is running the Android OS, like the Galaxy S3, or any other OS, speed is directly correlated.

For that reason, more processing power is better and all versions of the Galaxy S3 excel in that department. With multiple "cores" (a part of a CPU that can behave as a CPU by itself), either Quad core or Dual Core depending upon the phone's version, the S3 is expected to have top specifications well into late 2014.

Today there are no Apps available that will use a quad core chip to its fullest capacity and very few that even use dual cores. That is positive evidence in how much future proofing is built into this mobile.

The Galaxy S3's Graphics Capability

Due to quick shifting technology improvements, software and programs require intensive graphics that cannot be supplied by the computing device. This results in separate graphics cards being used to take the strain of enhanced graphical capabilities. The dedicated graphics chip of the S3 is one of the best examples of mobile graphics capability as this built in chip can match any graphics needs. The graphics chip is an integral part of the high end graphically demanding games, videos, intensive apps and multimedia that can run on the phone.

There is a slight difference between the two versions of the phone. The 4G LTE version has an Adreno 225 GPU on board whilst the international version sports the ARM Mali 400 MP graphics processing unit. Both are immensely capable of handling all sorts of graphics, the Mali 400 MP GPU provides complete 3D graphics acceleration up to 1080p. Unofficial tests have shown the GPU as being twice as fast as that of the S2. In addition to the graphics range the GPU's gives to video; gamers will find comparable graphics in mobile games on the S3 to those of modern day console gaming systems.

Without a good GPU, a device could only process a minimal amount of pixels, so one of the biggest advantages of a good GPU is that computerized images will have a lot more detail. The gap between what a console can deliver graphically and what the portable powerhouse in your pocket can do is now much, much narrower thanks to the combined power of the S3's graphics and CPU.

The Many Advantages of Syncing the Galaxy S3

The S3 has a huge amount of storage and even upgradeable memory in the form of Micro SD cards. However, is has also been designed with the ability to connect and share (sync), not only with your home PC, but also with more innovative Internet based syncing solutions. This provides alternate solutions to storage, and relieves the need to pack your phone with more memory.

Different Ways to Sync the S3

There are many software and hardware based ways to sync your S3. Being a Samsung manufactured product while running Google's Android operating system gives you the best of both worlds. Not only will you be able to save all information from a Google Account and keep that data backed up by Google's massive server farms, but you'll also have a Samsung account to access too. The S3 makes it amazingly simple to add any account that you want to keep synced with your phone. Most social networks, email and other account types can be added. Naturally, the most used functions like email and Facebook will be the most commonly synced accounts.

Samsung has even provided a solution for saving documents online. By owning the S3, you are granted access to "Dropbox" for two years and fifty Gb of data. Dropbox is an online "cloud based" storage that allows you to backup data such as photos and documents so that if your mobile is ever lost, you can retrieve your important information.

Additionally, you can consider using the syncing service from Samsung. The "Kies" service bills itself as "The Ultimate Media Library" and is Samsung's way of keeping all of your media files organized and in one place. Kies is a way of connecting and syncing your device with your laptop or home computer; is also supported by a new app called "Kies Air" that allows you to use Wi-Fi to manage content on your phone or desktop using a mobile browser.

The Benefits of Syncing

The most obvious benefit of regularly syncing your device is the security of your data. You may lose or break your S3, but your data will not be lost. With your Google account tracking your purchased and downloaded apps, you never need to worry about losing your apps. If you ever switch your mobile device (not sure why you would abandon the S3), all you would need to do is activate your existing Google account on the new device.

With existing data synced to a desktop or laptop, you'll have alternate ways and programs to manage your digital life. For example, you could start preparing a presentation on your phone on the way home from a daily commute and then seamlessly continue the work on your home machine. By using a system like "Dropbox", you could even start a document and give others permission to access it, allowing true multi user editing no matter where you are.

How Syncing Improves Productivity

Despite having one of the largest Smartphone screens and a great virtual keyboard, using a dedicated computer to do your work has some advantages. PCs usually boast a more accessible interface due to their traditionally larger screens and physical keyboards. Many people will choose to do the majority of their work on PCs, with the S3 standing by as the device of convenience to use for situations when booting up a computer is just not possible or convenient. Samsung understands this and that is why it's so easy and convenient to increase your productivity through syncing. Even simple actions such as Google syncing search history between devices can save so much time.

While businessmen and women can benefit the most from these high-end syncing functions, everyday users will get different utility. With your social accounts synced to S Planner, you will never miss an acquaintance's birthday. Just taking a quick look at S Planner will save you from remembering everyone's birthdays and special occasions.

Syncing Your Entertainment

The S3 is well regarded as one of the best mobiles for not only enjoying movies on, but also music and games. With this trinity of entertainment at your fingertips, syncing can once again solve a host of lost device type problems. There is no need to worry about losing any content downloaded from the Google Play market.

Anything downloaded from Google Play can not only be accessed on your own device using your Google Account, but any device that is eligible to use your account details. That means if you buy a movie from Google Play, you can start enjoying it on your phone and finish watching from your home computer. The Kies service from Samsung also provides functions to organize your entertainment. You can create and control playlists across multiple devices and services. Even your iTunes account can be synced using this method.

The Best Apps for the Galaxy S3

Having both the power of Samsung and Google, the S3 has both Google Play and Samsung's own "Samsung App Store" to download apps from. Here are some of the best apps in each category.

Entertainment Apps

IMDB is the premier Internet movie database, which translates fantastically to the 4.8 inch screen. Aside from the reviews, quotes, and trivia, the IMDB app provides local show times and allows for watching glorious HD trailers.

YouTube of course needs no introduction as the suppository of some of the best casual and entertaining video clips on the net. Once again, this mobile's larger screen shows its true power when playing your favorite viral videos over and over.

The Official Top 40 Chart is a Samsung exclusive app that gives you limited free access to the Top 40 Music charts. For a premium price, the songs can be bought and kept for personal use, but the initially free service provides unprecedented access to the top tunes of today.

Games

Games are certainly one type of app where the S3 will excel because of its high spec processing power. Here are some of the best games available for it.

Asphalt Racing 7: Heat is one of the best racing games by Gameloft. Continuing on a long running series, the latest game makes excellent use of the top end devices capabilities with some of the best near photo perfect graphics available in mobile gaming.

Shadowgun tries to bring the Sci-Fi over the shoulder shooter type game to mobile and does a fantastic job of it. Set in a futuristic mountain fortress, the intense 3rd person action combined with advanced artificial intelligence, advanced lighting effects, and console quality graphics makes it a must have for top end mobile gaming.

Samurai II Vengeance likens itself to a 3D console brawler, it has plenty of action and will run at 60 frames per second making it a gorgeously displayed game.

There are literally hundreds of games that could be recommended for the Galaxy S3 . To find out more of the best that mobile gaming has to offer, look to the bigger studios like Gameloft, EA and Glu Mobile who masterfully craft the top quality games.

Productivity

This mobile is a powerful business tool, and several apps are a must for those looking to unlock the S3's full potential.

Dropbox is a particular special app. With Samsung providing two years of 50Gb cloud storage via this service, is it the best method to having quick and easy access to all of your files and data. This app will save you hours of vital time that could be used in other areas of your business.

Google Drive can be considered the online standard for sharing, editing and storing documents. With the Android OS intrinsically linked to Google, it makes sense to download this app if you want better access to Google's virtual office software.

Although very similar, there are separate advantages of both services. One should see what works best for their needs, and many will find a great hybrid use of the two.

Apps for Children

Read Me Stories: Children's Books is one of the top free apps from the Samsung Store. With over 2 million worldwide readers this children's' app is very popular due to its ability to teach young people to read and with numerous free texts.

Kids Mode: Free Games + Lock is not only a suppository for apps that have been designated to be "Kid Friendly" but also provides a 'child-lock' that will keep the child in the app and prevent them from making any accidental purchases.

Other very good children friendly apps include Ant Smasher, 0-10 Numbers, Classic Simon and Talking Tom Cat (and its many variations).

Lifestyle Apps

Google Play is filled with many apps coming under the "Lifestyle" genre; many famous people and almost the entire spectrum of popular activities are presented there. At the moment these are the more popular Lifestyle Apps that take advantage of the S3's power:
Jamie's 20 Minute Meals, SAS Survival Guide and Barcode Scanner.

Another lifestyle app specifically made with this phone in mind is the S Health App. This is the start of a new wave of personal wellness apps and not only uses the device's many features, but is also compatible with many healthcare sensors such as blood glucose meters and body composition scales that it uses to improve and diagnose your health.

Other Apps to Consider

There are over 600,000 apps just available from the Google Play market. There are many other sources to download Android apps from and many apps are free. Samsung itself provides a very comprehensive app store dedicated to Galaxy S3 apps and games.

An occasional casual glance will often be rewarded by access to free apps of very high quality. As an example, at the time of writing Modern Combat 3: Fallen Nation despite being a high price from other sources is a free promotion on the Samsung market. If a user is ever overwhelmed by the sheer variety of apps, head to the "Apps selected by Samsung" category for some helpful direction.

Accessories for the Galaxy S3

Aside from the usual accessories that you can expect to buy for a cell phone, an entirely new item is available for this device and others with NFC (Near Field Communications) capability. Samsung TecTiles are reprogrammable stickers that use the NFC of your S3 to carry out phone functions. For example a TecTile can be attached to your bedside cabinet and programmed to set an alarm on the phone when the device is touches it. There are a broad spectrum of functions that they can be used for and are an entirely new category of accessory for modern mobiles.

Cases

The official case is the Galaxy S III Protective Cover Plus. It comes in a variety of colors, has a hard outer shell and a rubber bezel protecting the sides of the device. The raised lip of the bezel also provides drop protection for the screen. Naturally all ports and buttons are easily accessible.

For those wanting a little more protection there is also an official flip cover available. Currently sold with a marked down price as a bundle with 4 different colors (orange, pebble blue, light blue and green) the flip cover's hardback actually replaces your battery cover and the front then wraps around your phone to provide superior protection. Being an official product, full access to your device and its features is supported.

OtterBox provide an array of well-designed and sturdy cases; they're regarded as some of the most durable cases available. The OtterBox Commuter Case provides dual layer protection in the form of an inner silicone case and a hard outer polycarbonate shell. With a bundled screen protector and plugs to protect the ports, you're left with a sturdy case that doesn't make the phone unwieldy.

Batteries and Chargers for the S3

With the ability to change the battery simply by removing the cover it makes sense to buy a spare battery for your device if you plan to go on lengthy trips. Here is a selection of some of the more highly regarded batteries available:
For convenience and the surety that you're buying an authentic product we recommend getting the official Samsung Galaxy S3 2100 mAh battery. With the same specifications as the bundled battery, the official product can be found through most online retailers like Amazon.

Sometimes the day is just too long for your phone; if you find that you need a longer lasting battery the Mugen Power

4600mAh could be the power source for you. This battery available worldwide from Mugen Power Batteries retails at $98.95 but is worth the price as it will extend the length that you can use your device by approximately 2.19 times longer.

Zens Inductive Charger: The S3 is one of the few premium phones that is able to support a new technology known as inductive charging. This battery technology allows a phone to be powered without the use of messy cables cluttering up your work or living space. Zens provides a replacement battery cover for your phone, when the device is then placed on a charging mat (also supplied of course) it will immediately begin charging!

Docking Stations

Due to their popularity, there are a wide variety of docks for the S3. Android docks can be placed into two separate categories: Docks that are able to charge your mobile while listening to music or viewing movies and those which generally use wireless technology (normally Wi-Fi or Bluetooth) to stream media. Here are our top choices for the different types of docks that you might encounter.

Made by renowned company Neuros the Digital Innovations Universal Speaker Dock is arguably the World's first dedicated

Android dock. Not only will it charge your device but it also delivers exceptional music clarity. It is able to charge the phone through a USB connection and sound is ported through a headphone jack. Music apps such as Pandora and Amazon Cloud are supported with wireless remote control.

Philips is a company that has always been at the forefront of music technology. Their Philips AS531 Speaker soon made a name for itself as one of the most popular speaker docks. It has an on board battery for travel purposes and features noise blocking technology to eliminate mobile signal interference.

Another well know company is Creative Labs who in the past made some very high quality speakers for desktop computers. The sound quality is fantastic and the speaker itself has a very good build quality. The only drawback of their Creative D100 combined speaker and amplifier is that it works via Bluetooth , so won't be able to charge your S3 during use.

With your phone being a sturdy business tool you can't forget about the importance of having a good Bluetooth Car Kit. The Jabra Freeway Bluetooth In-Car Speakerphone comes highly recommended; the company has worldwide acclaim. It is the first in-car speakerphone that uses Virtual Surround sound. It also utilizes dual-mic technology to eliminate background noises, a crucial aspect for any sort of driving.

Samsung Galaxy S3 Versus the iPhone 5

When the iPhone 5 was recently announced, Galaxy S3 owners knew they had nothing to fear as their phone had been created using some of the finest mobile technology available. Here is how the two devices compare.

Dimensions

Naturally Apple saw the popularity of the larger screen and realized that with a bigger screen there's more convenience and entertainment value. Even so, at 4 inches compared to the impressive 4.8 inches of Samsung's device, there's been some disappointment from mobile community.

There's no denying that both of these are very light and slim phones. Apple's flagship is astonishingly light at 3.95 ounces and the extra screen size on the S3 increases the weight to 4.69 ounces. The fact that the iPhone is only 0.3 inches thick as opposed to the S3's 0.34 inches is superficially an advantage. However when you factor in the natural curved form of the S3, it seems that the straight, hard edges of the IPhone come out a second best to the more natural feel of the slightly bulkier Samsung handset.

Connectivity

One big problem of the IPhone is that it is plagued by a reliance on iTunes. So many media functions such as adding music and movies to an Apple phone need to be accessed via iTunes. As soon as you sync the IPhone with another ITunes account you're going to get that person's files and risk losing your own. Even straightforward sharing via conventional systems like Bluetooth is limited.

The Galaxy S3, on the other hand, actively encourages connecting with other devices and has a number of ways to do this. These include Bluetooth connectivity, AllShare Play, NFC and a variety of other ways.

For previous iPhone models, Apple had many 3rd party manufacturers of docks, speakers and accessories and an enormous amount of devices were created that fit the IPhone's 30-pin connector. But with the 5 there is a new type of connector, rendering any docks or other devices that people own useless.

The S3 on the other hand conforms to European legislation that has called for all modern mobiles to have USB or mini-USB connectivity. This means that it will play nicely with many tailored and generic devices, whether they be speakers, other Android chargers or docking stations.

Memory

For reasons only known to Apple (although some put it down to greed and design constraints) none of their mobile products have ever had the ability to use external memory such as a SD card. Despite this, for most purposes the sizes of on-board memory, in the form of 16, 32 or 64 GB storage devices should be enough for most users.

However, with media increasing in size due to HD formats and app/games becoming ever larger, those limits could easily prove to be constraining. The S3 is more versatile in the memory department; current available devices have fixed 16 or 32Gb storage (with a 64Gb variant planned to be released shortly).

Unlike the iPhone 5, however, this onboard memory can be shored up with micro SD storage. A phone with 128 GB capacity thus would trump the iPhone's storage capabilities. There's also the cloud based Dropbox storage that Samsung provides for free.

Camera

The newest iPhone 5 camera has already attracted some negative press. It has been reported that many of the first phones sold have reported a 'Purple Haze' around the photos in certain lighting conditions. Aside from possible design flaws the camera is a solid 8 Megapixel shooter with a backlit sensor.

However, the main enhancements over the previous version are the software improvements. The S3 also has an 8 Megapixel camera but it could be argued that there is a slightly sturdier build to this one with few reports of any technical or hardware-related faults.

Both the phones feature a panoramic mode and various ways to edit photos. Despite many similarities, many users prefer the S3 camera because of the added Social sharing features and innovations like "Face Tag" that can detect and label the faces of your friends.

Battery

The winner both specification wise and performance wise when it comes to battery power is the Galaxy S3. The Android phone's battery has a greater capacity and in most tests outperforms the iPhone. With one battery lasting almost two days in some cases and the other needing nightly charging (with only the negligible improvement over the 4S' battery capability) the difference is obvious.

When you factor in the ability of an S3 user to be able to swap batteries (a simple task that takes under a minute) as opposed to the IPhone 5's inaccessible battery, it's clear Samsung wins this category.

The New Samsung Mini S3

Android fans had a pleasant surprise recently when a new Galaxy phone was released. The Galaxy S3 Mini came out enjoying many of the attributes of the original, but also addressing some issues that deterred a few buyers from the getting the larger handset.

Basic Features

- The Mini has a 5Mp camera with a LED Flash, this is supported by a front facing VGA camera.

- FM Radio function is supported.

- The latest version of Android, 4.1 Jelly bean is already running on the mobile.

- An extremely fast processor powers the phone: The Dual Core 1Ghz St-Ericsson Chip is comparable to many current generation chips

- The size has many smaller handed users delighted: It measures in at a very slim 111.5 g and the dimensions are 121.55 x 63 x

9.85 mm. It has excited a lot of people that it is actually lighter than the much more expensive iPhone 5

- The large 1,500 mAh battery provides excellent talk and standby time

- There are numerous ways to connect to other devices and services. These include NFC, Bluetooth and Wi-Fi

- The screen is simply beautiful. Using Samsung's best WVgA Super Amoled screen, you'll always have a sharp and colorful picture with good hues and contrasts and statistics demonstrate the phone's clarity: 800 x 480 pixels with 233 PPI (pixels per inch)

- Internal memory storage should be more than enough for most users needs with the Mini coming in 8 and 16 GB varieties. If you ever find the need to increase the memory capacity a Micro SD card is compatible up to 32GB.

- With access to the Google Play store and its hundreds of thousands of apps, every owner will be more than happy with the diverse array of app's available to the phone. But there is also access to many other Google services that truly make this mobile device great.

Google Search is fully supported and Google Now supports the latest Jelly bean OS. You'll never have a lack of entertainment options, as there are countless games, books, and movies available on the Google Play store.

YouTube enjoys native support on the Mini allowing access to millions of video clips. And if you want to leave the confines of your home and visit a real movie theater, Google Navigation combined with Places will quickly guide you to the best destination.

Aside from the slick touch screen that uses multi-finger touch there are various sensors that can be used to control the device too. Proximity sensors are used to perform functions such as muting the device when placed face down and calling contacts when the device senses it is being held up to ear level.

The accelerometer has numerous ways it can be used; chief among these is control of a multitude of apps and the handy ability to turn the phone from landscape into portrait mode. There is even a compass function if Google Maps should ever let you down.

Advantages Over the Original S3

The original S3 is very much a premium handset and whether you are purchasing it outright or using it on contract you can expect to pay a fairly handsome amount. The Mini has most of the features of the S3 but has a slightly more wallet friendly price. Typically you can expect to pay about $400 for a Mini but will be adding on an extra $200 to buy the larger phone.

The Mini already runs Android 4.1 Jelly Bean OS; many countries across the World and including North America are still awaiting the update to Jelly Bean for the S3. This update might be many months away for some networks and will naturally come with teething problems. This isn't the case with the smaller version of the mobile as it has been thoroughly tested prior to release with Jelly Bean being the stock OS.

It's quite obvious that everybody doesn't have the same sized hands. That's why despite being a fantastic device the S3 is not for everybody. The Samsung Galaxy S3 Mini addresses this problem with its smaller and slimmer profile. You'll be able to enjoy similar performance but the smaller form will mean that one-handed use becomes much easier. The more ergonomic and unobtrusive size means that it is much easier to squeeze into a jeans pocket or a small handbag.

Get the Most Out of Your Samsung Galaxy S3

The last thing you want is your powerful mobile to run out of juice when you're away from home. We've compiled a few little tips on how to get the most out of your battery. Naturally, the biggest drain on battery power is that luscious screen. In your settings you can change display options.

An automatic brightness setting is available that will vary the screens brightness according to the latent light around you. This alone will make a difference to your battery's longevity , but the phone has a further "Power Saving" option that can be accessed. This power saving can be tweaked to use minimal CPU power, screen power and other power saving measures.

For a new user you might often wonder what all the LED notifications are indicating. The S3 has a few LED based cues that are not widely understood. Known as the "service light", you can typically expect to see three different colors. A blue light shows missed events such as calls, notifications and messages. A flashing red light will show that your battery is low. And expect to see a green light when the phone is connected to a charger and is fully charged. The green light will also show up if you're surfing the net and the phone goes into standby mode.

Of course you're going to want to have many great apps on your device. Luckily there is a way to conveniently sort these apps for easy access. The Touchwiz UX interface that is used allows easy alphabetical sorting of apps. Just select the Apps Drawer, now press the Menu button and choose "Alphabetical Grid".

Gesture controls make life much easier; some of the most convenient ones allow quick and easy ways to communicate with people in your contacts list. Go into contacts and then with simple swipes your friends can be messages or called. Swipe left to right across your contact to place a call or right to left to message them!

The built in Driving Mode can also prove useful not just on the road, but in everyday situations. By enabling text to speech and activating driving mode many useful notifications are read aloud to you: incoming call, message, new emails, new voicemail, alarm, schedule and unlock screen. That means when you're driving, the phone will tell you who's calling or messaging. Another useful feature will tell you who just sent you a text message and if you should reply immediately or later on.

Never miss a photo opportunity again! The camera app can be quickly accessed using motion control. If the phone is locked, just hold a finger on the screen and rotate the device to open the camera. A similar trick can be used to access other apps from the lock screen. Instead of swiping across the screen to unlock just hold and swipe the desired app. If you get it right then the phone will unlock on that app.

Unfortunately there are very few mobile providers that have unlimited data plans any more. You have the ability to take control of your data usage by going into Settings and selecting Data Usage. Now choose the "Set mobile data limit" and you will be able to see how much data is being used and set a cap on maximum use.

The Android Ice-Cream operating system on the S3 is very intuitive and has a lot of great features. But already in some parts of the World this is being updated with the Jelly bean OS that provides a number of benefits, chief amongst them being the ability to use the new Google Now service.

If your handset hasn't updated yet, a simple sync with the desktop version of Samsung Kies will show if you are using the latest software. Some mobile carriers in many regions, notably North America, are currently delaying the update.

If you ever find that you are using the handset during a normal working day and are running short on battery, some steps can be taken to prolong the battery life. The easiest method is to use the "power saving" mode accessed from the top pull down menu. This can be tinkered with to help lower consumption. You also need to consider turning off features like Wi-Fi and GPS. These two are big battery drainers and if not being used can quickly be turned off, again from the top pull down menu.

www.ingramcontent.com/pod-product-compliance
Lightning Source LLC
Chambersburg PA
CBHW071032050326
40689CB00014B/3627